THE BRIGHT SIDE
OF REJECTION

(When no means yes)

Victor Ibeh

Victor Ibeh asserts his right to be identified as the author of this work

© **Victor Ibeh, 2017**

Cover design by Fehintoluwa C. Ogunyemi

ISBN 9781973100126

DEDICATION

For my Son Victor Ibeh Jnr., who didn't get a chance to live....
13/11/2013 – 09/04/2015

For my friend Ukeje Emmanuel.

For my friend Catherine Channah.

For my Mother, Ruth Ibe.

Other books by Victor Ibeh

Voice of Wisdom

Voice of wisdom is a potpourri of evolutionary and thought-provoking insights to the world of wisdom, designed to help you discover the pathway to success in your mind and depend on your personal abilities. The journey to self-fulfillment is such that you cannot successfully embark on without the subliminal presence of your mind. This book would help you utilize the creative energy of your mind and reach your desired destination.

Emotional Insurance

People do all within their power to protect themselves from all kinds of harm but very little attention is paid to their emotions. They carry on their emotional transactions with recklessness. Only after there has been hurt, do they pause to wish, they had done things aright.This book is coming in handy for all those who seek......."

Festered wounds.

"Everyday, in the course of daily activities, we sustain injuries. Unfortunately, not everybody gets to heal. The problem most times isn't the injuries sustained but what we do about them. This has led to a lot of people living with festered wounds and endangering their lives....."

CONTENT

AUTHOR'S NOTE

Thank you for picking up this book. It is my desire that you will find the healing and freedom you deserve. By the time you are through with this book, you will find out that rejection does not have as much power as you have always thought.

The idea is to demystify rejection and give you power over it. We must identify with rejection as an integral part of our existence. By so doing, we won't get hurt when it occurs. Instead, we will learn the lessons it brings and move on. You will be glad that you invested in this book.

Join me and take this walk to mental, psychological and emotional freedom.

INTRODUCTION

It was in my 4th year in the University that I experienced a certain rejection that made me suicidal. The lady I loved, came up one morning and told me that it was over between us.

There was no previous disagreement. We both travelled for a short holiday and came back to school. I came back before her, so, the day she came back I couldn't see her. The next morning during lectures, she called me and asked that I meet her in the lobby of our faculty. I got there and she greeted me. After exchanging pleasantries, she told me that she was no longer interested in our relationship. I didn't see it coming. I was shocked. I asked her for the reason behind her decision. She told me she had none and was not willing to discuss it. She stood up and walked away.

I began to call her line but she wasn't taking my calls. I freaked out. Went back to my lecture hall. Picked up my books and walked out of the hall. I wasn't thinking straight. Tears filled my eyes and were strolling down my face. People saw me as I walked out of the faculty and might probably have thought I lost a loved one to death, but, I actually lost a loved one, just that it wasn't to death.

I felt worthless. I felt life had no more meaning. I boarded a bus home. When I got home I went to the market and bought poison to drink myself to death. I had already built my future around her. I didn't see the possibility that I could get someone else in my life.

I got the poison and went home. The thought propelling me to commit suicide was that my life was useless and meaningless without her. I kept asking myself what I would do without her.

I wrote a suicide note and kept on my reading table. I was in tears. It felt like my heart was being ripped apart. I thought of my future and I felt bad that my future was never going to be. At the very last minute, my pastor called me on the phone and asked that I see him in his office. The reason I responded to his call was because he was somebody I respected so much, at that time. I kept back the poison and got dressed and went to see my pastor. I got there and from my look he knew something was wrong. So, he asked. I narrated what happened, to him. He spent some time talking to me and encouraging me to let it go and face my studies. I didn't even tell him about my suicide plans. By the time he finished talking with me, I was still hurt but I didn't feel like committing suicide any longer.

I have had other rejection experiences after that particular experience. I will still have more. I made peace with it. It is part of our existence here.

Not everybody is lucky to stay alive after a rejection. I have read about people who killed themselves and the people they claimed to love. On Facebook, we have read about young men and women who committed suicide after a rejection. Sadly, some even committed suicide live on Facebook video application. I recall the story of the lady that jumped to her death in 2015 after she caught her husband having sex with her mother. She couldn't handle it and she committed suicide.

Part of the reason we have many cases of depressed people today, is that they are slaves to rejection. People who are slaves to rejection suffer depression after they have been rejected. All that, is about to change for you. After reading this book you will discover what nobody has ever told you about rejection.

You will learn to master your emotions and stop feeling bad about rejection. There is so much to learn from the pages of this book, that you will find it to be an invaluable resource. Every human should have a copy of this book. We can heal the world if we all have this book and learn from it.

CHAPTER ONE

WHEN DARKNESS STRIKES

WHEN DARKNESS STRIKES

Have you ever been told these words, No, go away, I don't want you, I hate you etc? These words convey an enormous amount of negative energy that can shatter even the most powerful human. The devastating effect of that is not just physical - It affects the psychological and emotional being of the Person who receives it.

Irrespective of how mild, polite and seemingly harmless the words or actions of rejection may be constructed or displayed, rejection is a bitter pill to taste. It doesn't at anytime taste sweet to the recipient except the recipient had no pre-interest in the object of rejection- in which case it cannot be referred to as rejection.

Rejection is a very prominent feature of human cycles of existence. This is because personality, character, wishes, desires, interests, choices, decisions etc vary. We are not all the same. We thrive on personal differences and uniqueness. No two people are the same. This also makes a case for the differences in the choices they make. Because what A wants most of the times wouldn't be what B wants. This also gives credence to the saying, "one man's meat is another man's poison".

Rejection occurs daily in human affairs. Rejection is a part of our daily lives. We experience it in the Church, Market, workplace, relationships, marriages, etc. The effects are quite devastating, heart-rendering and ego crumbling. You can't always control the frequency at which you get rejected. You can only choose how to respond to it, to avoid empowering it against yourself.

You are going to reject people, and you will also be a victim of rejection. It is a two-way traffic. Sometimes, rejection is inevitable. In most cases you might try to be sympathetic but the magnitude of the choice, specifications and decisions you have to make, would drown every will in you to accept that person. You end up rejecting him/her not because you really wish to but because you are limited in choice. The person being rejected in such instance, would just be a victim of happenstance. This rejection is not motivated by ill will. Not all cases of rejection come from an intention to hurt. Some are unavoidable or inadvertent, but they happen all the same.

Rejection sometimes could be as a result of third-party interference. If the person rejecting you is subject to another person's authority or influence, he /she may reject you not because they really want to but because of external influence. This was the case of a lady who had been in romantic relationship with a man for seven years. They were meant to tie the nuptial knot shortly after the seventh year but their whole plan flopped. The parents of the young man opposed the plan on the basis that the lady was from a certain tribe which they disliked. The young man in his bid to please his parents and not lose their marriage blessings, broke off the relationship and left the lady heartbroken.

The effect of that rejection was so much for the lady that she attempted suicide but by a stroke of luck, she was rescued and taken to a medical center where she was stabilized and treated. Thereafter, she sought for the services of a therapist for therapy and healing. The rejection in her case was motivated by a third party. This is just an isolated case.

The truth is that rejection can have very damaging effects on a person's life if it is not properly managed. Though, rejection in itself is powerless. Our reaction to it, and how it affects us is where the power lies. Our self-esteem at the moment of the rejection can influence how it affects us.

CHAPTER TWO

WHAT IS REJECTION?

WHAT IS REJECTION?

Rejection is a very heavy word that sends shivers down the spine of anybody that hears it. The moment you talk about rejection, everybody comes up with a story of an experience. We all have something to say about rejection.

Rejection is a feeling of disappointment that comes when your expectations are dashed. The effects of rejection is purely emotional/psychological. This is why it would be erroneous to categorize it into types. For instance, I see people say things like: financial rejection, emotional rejection, family rejection etc. Rejection is rejection.

TYPES OF REJECTION

Rejection affects every aspect of your life. It affects you emotionally/psychologically, though, there is an emotion-based rejection. This is the type that comes from romantic transactions. But, it will be wrong to classify rejection by saying that the types of rejection are: emotional rejection, financial rejection, matrimonial rejection etc.

Whichever way you experience rejection, the effect must be emotional/psychological.

This is why people suffer depression after losing a job opportunity, academic opportunity, romantic breakup, family rejection; all these affect us all emotionally and psychologically. This is because every type of rejection, affects you majorly at the emotional/psychological realm. There are other places they would affect you, though, but, it all ends at your emotional threshold.

You will think about the rejection and you will feel bad/hurt. In some cases you might want to do something terrible to yourself. All these happen in your mind. Yes, rejection, can affect your bank account. It can affect your business or other aspects of your life. But, the basic place where you feel the impact – where the evaluation takes place, is your mind. This is why my focus is on your emotional wellbeing. Remember, they say, "a hungry man is an angry man". Inasmuch as the stomach is facing challenges, it is the emotions, that feel the impact. If a hungry man evaluates his situation and decides to find a way to deal with his hunger, it won't drain him emotionally. However, there is the hungry man who will not do anything about finding a solution. Instead, he will sit at a place and get angry and transfer aggression to people around him – thus becoming a danger to himself and other people. This is a typical example of when the emotions suffers for something happening in other areas of your life.

For rejection, it is the same. Not all rejections come from romantic dealings. Some are a product of other aspects of our daily activities. Yet, the effect is usually felt in our emotions.

Emotion-based rejection

This is rejection that comes from romantic activities. Humans are always interested in romantic relationships. This might be within or outside the confines of matrimony. We always have that desire for someone to be exclusively ours. Someone we love and care about. Someone we share intimacy with – physically, sexually, abstractly, and in all ways conceivable.

Romance is beautiful. Some people like to think that romance is all about touching the opposite or same sex, in ways that would only lead to erotic exchange. This isn't so. Romance can be practised through actions, words, touch, and every way that we interact. The call to romance is always made when we convince ourselves that we are in love with someone. Even among animals, there is the courtship behavior which can be equated to the art of romance in humans. Romance shows that someone is the recipient of your exclusive emotional interest. You want that person. You do not care about other people. Something melts in your heart when you think about such person.

From mere interest, you take it a step forward by disclosing how you feel, to know if that person shares your feelings and interests. Now, understand that you are the one interested. The person you are interested in, may not want you. They may not feel anything for you. Do you think it is wrong for them not to feel anything for you? Do you think it is compulsory, that your feeling for them will be mutual? Of course not. Humans are free moral agents. You cannot force anybody to desire what they don't want to desire. How will you handle it when that person you have fantasized about, created a mental future with, and visualized in your life, says "No" to you? Is it everybody you see on the road that you desire? Do you catch random feelings for everybody you meet in life?

Now think about it. If you do not catch feelings for everybody you meet, why do you think other people must do same for you? Does it not occur to you that they actually have a right to choose who they want in life, just as we have "Menu" in eateries. Nobody forces you to eat what you don't feel like eating. Think about the vast multitudes of people in the world. It should show you that there is room for people to make choices out of a range of options. Every human has the right to choice.

This is just an instance, coming from romantic relationship outside matrimony. Understand that the proposal from you to the person you are proposing to, might be for marriage, short term romance, sex, etc. it could be for anything. We are not concerned at this moment with the motive behind it. What is of utmost importance is that romance-based rejection can happen either within a marriage or outside a marriage.

There is also the rejection that comes during the existence of the romantic relationship. Apart from the very rare case of lovers who reach a unanimous agreement to break up a relationship – in which case we might not call it rejection, since it is mutual and not triggered by one person's selfish interest. Some lovers can get to a point where they agree that the relationship is not working, probably, as a result of some fundamental issues of compatibility. It may also be health-related. Under such circumstance, none of the parties would claim to have been heartbroken by the other, unless of course there was some mischief whereby one party dealt fraudulently with the other.

People can get to a point in their romantic journey where one party decides to walk out of the relationship. He/she may give or not give a legitimate reason for walking out. Whether the reason is legitimate or not, doesn't matter much in this case. What matters is that there is rejection and you have to deal with it. My interest is not to pet you with words. I am interested in opening your eyes to reality. This is to protect you from being expectant that all your rejections would come with legitimate explanations. If you build yourself that way, when someone rejects you in the course of a relationship without a so-called legitimate reason, it will break you down and put you in a very difficult position. I like to prepare you for the worst case scenario to get equipped in case things turn out messy.

So, if your partner walks out on you in the course of a relationship, will you end your life? Will you harm that partner? Will you spend the rest of your life bemoaning your experience? None of these should be your reaction. You should know that anybody has the right to walk out of any relationship at any point in life. It is immaterial that you are treating him/her right. What matters is that they are actually making use of their legitimate right to choice. Romantic relationship, is not enslavement. When you truly love people, you should also accommodate the possibility that they could wake up and leave you any day.

In as much as you wish to stay together forever, always leave room for change. Leave room for them to walk away when they choose to. It is actually better for a partner to walk away than to make your life miserable as a result of dissatisfaction. This is perhaps one of the reasons that should make you learn the right way to love. If you love the right way, you will hardly have much loss to count if a partner decides to walk. Also, you should be reminded that you might be the one who wants to walk out of a relationship. Do you think your partner should harm you for making use of your own right? I bet you will say no.

There is another form of rejection that occurs within matrimony. This is similar to the above mentioned form of emotion-based rejection. The only difference is that the former occurs outside a marriage, while the latter occurs in marriage. People actually think that marriage gives emotional immunity. But, does it? It doesn't. Marriage is just a union. It doesn't change people. The good thing about marriage in some cases is legal protection. Outside that, you are dealing with the same humans.

A spouse can wake up one day and decide that he or she is tired of the marriage. It doesn't have to be because you did anything wrong to him/her. It is the power of choice. I know most people get into marriage, believing that they are emotionally secure for life. Nothing could be farther from the truth. This explains why it shatters them when their supposed eternal partner decides to take a walk. I am trying so hard to avoid mentioning the instances where the rejection occurs as a result of something wrong that a partner has done or is doing to the other partner. This rejection, may not come in form of an end to the marriage. It may start with something as little as, refusal to spend time together, engage in sexual activities, poor communication, stinginess etc. all these are precursors to something bigger – which could be a divorce or separation. How do you handle such unanticipated situation?

For all it is worth, this is rejection staring you in the face. Rejection has come to roost in your marriage. The same marriage where vows were made. Oh! You didn't know humans can break their vows? But, of course we break vows all the time. When was the last time you broke a vow you made to someone? Have you ever failed a promise? Then, you should also know that the next human can break a vow. It is immaterial that it was a vow taken in church or registry or before custodians of native customs. Humans can break vows at anytime. When they do, how will you handle it?

Family-based rejection

Family-based rejection occurs within the family unit. There is no need mentioning the type of family in this discourse. Whatever the word family means to you, just know that rejection occurs therein. Being members of the same family, is no proof that you cannot experience rejection in one another's hands.

I already mentioned, that we have different interests and desires. This also plays out in the family setting. We don't always want the same things. At the point where our various interests are at variance with one another, rejection will find its way into our lives. It will become necessary that somebody must reject the other, in order to get what he/she wants.

Children suffer rejection, in the hands of their parents. There are children who suffered rejection even from the point of conception. This might perhaps, be the worst form of family rejection. In this case, the child hasn't been given a chance to be good or bad, at least for the rejection to have some sort of validity. How on earth do you resent an unborn child? A child that didn't do anything to bring about his/her conception. It is a case of people shamelessly running away from responsibility. A child is usually a product of two adults, male and female. The child has no control over it. It is sad that these same adults would transfer whatever angst they have for each other to the child who is the product of their own indiscretion. Then, you see the child already facing the realities of a cruel world even before birth. Tell me again about rejection in its very ugly form.

Most children suffer rejection from deadbeat and absentee fathers. Some of these fathers reject the children from the time of pregnancy.

They sometimes claim not to be responsible for the pregnancy. The other group are those who vanish after child delivery. You see them following after other women and abandoning the mother of their children. This is why we have a lot of single mothers in the society today. Most of the children being raised by single mothers are already victims of rejection from their fathers.

Parents also suffer rejection in the hands of their children. Like I already stated, we all experience rejection in different ways, there is nobody who has never had rejection experiences. It is part of our existence as humans.

Parents can suffer rejection in the hands of their children and vice versa. It would have made sense to say that children only reject their parents when the children have grown into adulthood and probably feel resentful towards their parents for something those parents did to hurt them. Some parents are very cruel to their children. They treat them like slaves. Some fathers are guilty of this. Mothers too, but in most cases, fathers are usually the culprits of this negative attitude. They come so hard on their children until the children can't handle it any longer.

This is the case of most rejected parents. Some parents maltreat their children to the point where those children develop bitterness toward them. This usually occurs in those days when the children are completely dependent on their parents. If such parents do not treat their children with love and care, there is every tendency that the children will become resentful and the moment they gain some sort of independence, they would reject their parents. The rejection in this case can be said to be legitimate. We can argue that the parents deserve it. This however, does not make it any less of a harrowing experience. While we may not be making a case in favour of such parents, there is need to highlight that some parents actually do some of those things ignorantly, because they lack basic knowledge needed for parenting.

This situation is very common in Africa, because the style of parenting is different from what is obtainable in the western world. African parents are entitled and feel like they are gods over their children. They hardly take the feelings of their children into consideration. It is all about them. It wouldn't be much of a surprise to see African parents in their old, senile and dependent age, being abandoned by their children. Most of them are suffering the effects of their actions in their earlier years.

There are also cases of parents forcing their own selfish interests on their children. We must understand that children have a mind of their own. It is abusive to attempt to use your children to live out your life. You should let them live their own lives. If a parent keeps forcing his/her will on a child, it will get to a point where that child rejects such parent. This rejection will come from the innate desire of every human to pursue their basic interests. The children might not have the will and power to say "no" to their parents at that point, but with time they would find the freedom they seek and their next action will be to reject their parents.

Not all cases of children rejecting their parents are occasioned by the wrongful action of parents. Some children develop rejection for their parents at a tender age. There are children who just resent both or one of their parents. It is not as a result of anything the parent has done. It just happens. This is another proof that children have a mind of their own. Else, why would a child of five just resent a parent who hasn't done any particular thing to hurt him/her? Perhaps, we could call this, one of the mysteries of life.

Rejection from siblings is another form of rejection that exist in families. There are so many cases of sibling's rejection, in families. One of the root causes of this is the introduction of divide and rule principle and favoritism by parents. The moment a parent or both parents, starts showing traits that they value one child above others, they have laid the foundation of rejection in their home. The siblings who are less preferred are naturally going to gang up and be resentful towards the favored child. This was exactly the experience of the biblical Joseph in the hands of his siblings.

The circumstances of birth can also lead to

rejection. If a man for instance, gets a child outside his marriage, there is every tendency for the children within the home to resent that child. Except in cases where conscious effort is made by the man and the wife in the home to maintain love and harmony among those children, there is bound to be friction in their relationships, thereby creating room for rejection. The biblical Jephthah had this experience. This is part of why it is advisable that parents make adequate arrangement for children before they are born. It is one thing to have an affair as a married person, and another thing to let that affair bring about a love child.

We will not overlook the possibility of rejection that can arise through divorce. After a divorce where there are children, both spouses can proceed to marry other people. It is no surprise, that the new union can lead to children. If care is not taken, the children from the previous marriage can suffer rejection in the hands of the children from the current marriage, and vice versa.

Some siblings just wouldn't get along with

themselves. Usually, it isn't because there has been anything wrong, done by either of the siblings. They just find out that they don't get along. We all have that one sibling we just don't like. From a mild dislike, it could grow into full rejection, where we don't care about them at all. This is the point where we treat them with disrespect and in some cases humiliate them.

We have that sibling who is a constant thorn in the flesh of others, usually, an elder who is entitled and thinks the younger siblings owe him/her anything. If that sibling continues with such nasty attitude, chances are, that resentment would build up and the other siblings would have no choice but to reject him/her.

In extended families, rejection occurs among cousins, between uncles/aunts and nephews/nieces, grand parents and grand children. These are all realities that we cannot pretend that they don't exist.

Finally, under family rejection, there is a very common form of rejection which exist between a wife/husband and the family of their spouse.

Some women suffer rejection from their parents-in-law and siblings-in-law all the days of their marriage. The men also experience this. This accounts for quite an impressive number of broken marriages today.

Most parents haven't learnt to allow their children make their choices of life partners. They complicate the lives of their children by trying to impose their own choices on their children. This is abusive. It is sad that they have nobody to tell them the truth. It is totally abusive for parents to limit the power of their children to make marital choices. Children who have become adults should be given a free hand to make their choices of a life partner.

Marriage is strictly the business of those in it. The best you can do for your children is to advise them, but the ultimate choice should be made by them, and every responsible parent is expected to respect the choices of their children.

You might not know it, but, interfering in the choices of your children, has far-reaching consequences. You end up complicating, not just the life of your own child but also the life of their intended spouse. In situations where the child goes ahead to settle down with their choice spouse, they will expose that spouse to rejection from family. This naturally would make life unbearable for that spouse. One single act of selfishness by parents, can ruin the lives of so many people. This doesn't look like a life worth living. Perhaps, we could minimize this if parents learnt to respect boundaries. But will African parents learn?

Finance-based rejection

Money they say, answers to everything. This might be why people chase after money like their whole lives depend on it – or maybe their whole lives actually depend on it.

To this end, it will be safe to say that rejection can be finance-based. Something as powerful as money should be able to bring about rejection.

One of the ways that you can suffer rejection, financially, is when you solicit for financial gifts and you are turned down. This could be from family members, friends, colleagues, random strangers etc. Usually, the reason for which you need that money would determine who you would ask from. We all have different reasons for needing money. Whether it is for something reasonable or unreasonable, what matters is that when you are turned down, you will definitely get hurt.

The most important ingredient here is "desire". As long as it is something you truly desire, when you ask and you fail to receive, you will feel bad. Our concern here, is not to determine if the desire was legitimate or not. Have you seen a baby trying to play with something dangerous. If you take that harmful object from the child, it will start crying. What is important there is the fact that there is a desire. This is also applicable to adults when they want money for something. Even if they want to use that money for something wrong, it will not change the fact that they would feel bad when they are refused.

Another way you can experience finance-based rejection, is when you request for loans. Let's not bother about who you are asking the loan from. It is enough that you made a request because you want it. You will feel bad.

In the first and second instances I just gave, the way to deal with this sort of rejection is to avoid having "entitlement mentality". Nobody owes you anything, just as you owe nobody anything. People get mad when you refuse to oblige them because they are filled with all sorts of "entitlement mentality". When you ask people for financial assistance, and they can't help, you have no reason being mad at them. It is their money. You have no right being mad at them.
Even if they are people you have helped in the past. Remember that helping them was a voluntary act on your part. You should also respect their own decision to help you or not. I know this is difficult to digest but it is the reality. Instead of getting mad and harming yourself in the process, you should rather make alternative arrangements. Seek for ways to get what you want. Don't depend on only one source. Always seek out multiple options.

Another way you can also experience finance-based rejection is when a debtor refuses to repay a loan. There are some people who lack integrity to repay loans. This class of people, will insult you for demanding your own money. It is natural for you to feel hurt when they fail to keep their promises of repaying the loan at a specific time period.

In a situation where you need that money to deal with a specific project in your life, it is not a surprise that their failure to repay that loan can affect you emotionally. How do you get past this? Will you go ahead and harm yourself by being sad and angry? It won't be the best action in such circumstance. Whatever you do at that point, you must avoid extreme emotions that can hurt.

When giving loans to people, wisdom should be applied. Avoid giving loans to friends and family. If you must give loans to family and friends, give them money that you can consider as a gift and forget it. It is tough recovering debts from friends and family. Most of the time, you end up as sworn enemies. It is better you don't give at all. If they decide to resent you, the loss won't be double. If you loan them money and they fail to repay you, you end up losing both the money and their friendship. The painful part of this is that you will also be hurt emotionally, because the failure to recover that debt is also rejection. Finance-based rejection can either be from not getting money from other people or recovering your money from those owing you.

Job-related rejection.

This form of rejection is very common. It is occasioned by the need to have a source of income, subject to certain laid down principles.

There are two major ways that this occurs. Rejection that is job-related can occur when a potential employer turns down your request for a job. Conversely, it can also occur when a potential employee turns down a job offer from an employer. Another way it can occur is when an employer relieves an employee of his/her job. As long as it is not based on mutual agreement, where both parties have nothing to lose, it will be safe to say that rejection has occurred. It may also be the employee who resigns from his/her job. This is a rejection experience for the employer, considering that it would definitely destabilize operations in the work environment.

As sad as this may sound, we can't prevent these things from happening. They are a part of our existence. In a work environment, people will come in and some people would go. People come into our lives daily and people leave too.

When you apply for a job, you should know that you might get that job or you might not. Nothing is cast in stone. Even if your qualifications are in sync with what the establishment wants, there might be other factors that would deter you from getting that job. Avoid malice. It also doesn't mean you are not good enough. It is one of life's experiences.

Avoid defining yourself based on that experience. Even if it is more than one or two experiences, it still doesn't define you. You must see the positive side of every rejection experience. Some people who fail to secure jobs, end up becoming entrepreneurs and employers.

You must understand that your failure to secure a job doesn't reduce who you are. Don't let it affect how you see yourself. Sometimes, you need such experiences to awaken you to other alternatives.

CHAPTER THREE

PROCESS OF REJECTION

PROCESS OF REJECTION

A particular form of rejection can be a one time experience, periodic or continuous. Some people don't know that rejection isn't just about being heartbroken from a breakup.

One time rejection

Some rejection experience can take a one-time approach. This mode of rejection occurs frequently. In fact it is an everyday affair. People face this rejection, each day they wake up from sleep.

The market person who calls out to a potential client to buy her goods and gets rejected, the man who woos a woman and she declines, the woman who professes her love to a man and he turns her down, the job seeker who applies for a job without being shortlisted for an interview, the parent who refuses to give their child(ren) what they ask for, etc. The list is endless. We suffer it daily. It takes that simple form of "No", "I can't", "we can't employ you" etc. As simple and seemingly harmless these words may appear, they have changed the course of the lives of so many people. This change might be positive or negative. For those who understand, they turn the experience into an inspiration for something good. The others who lack that ability become victims and never recover from the experience.

This one-time rejection is more common because it is direct and not subtle, unlike other modes. This mode scares people a lot. People are filled with the fear of receiving a "no" for an answer.

Women in this clime, hardly woo men. They claim that traditionally, men are meant to woo women. I agree with them to an extent, but this is not completely true. The times have changed. The message of gender equality is sweeping across this clime. People are becoming more aware that men and women are essentially equal and should be given equal treatment. This is in our bid to minimize and totally eradicate gender-based discrimination and all forms of ill treatment being given to the supposedly lesser gender – women. What this also means is that women now understand that they have a right to desire any man of their choice. They are not just going to sit still and wait until a man comes for them. We are meant to interact equally in the society. Women therefore, have a right to woo any man of their choice. The worst he can do is say no. In my opinion, "no" shouldn't be so much of a death sentence. When you see women saying that they can't woo men, the real fear is the fear of rejection. They can't handle it. There is a subtle romance of entitlement mentality in this issue. Women believe that men should woo them, and that they have the right to play around and do all the "shakara" before saying an ultimate "yes" if the man is someone they truly want. This is a very wrong teaching. It takes away a sense of responsibility from them. This is also why they find it difficult wooing men. They are scared of being rejected.

If women can desire any man, then it is not out of place for them to woo that man they desire. The traditional position that women are to be wooed by men, compulsorily, loses its power the moment a woman desires a man. This is because the power to desire is also the power to go for that which is desired. If women consider themselves free to desire men, they should also feel free to woo such men. The idea that a woman has to be wooed is limiting in itself. What about a woman who doesn't get a man to woo her? Oh! She would probably be seen as one having some spiritual problems that would require the prayers of a preacher. You see where this leads to. Women who have never had a man woo them, are likely to think that something is wrong with them. Then, they would go about looking for some solutions that really don't exist. What a sad situation! Whereas, a simple, "Hi Tom, I would love a date with you, at your convenience......" could have saved that situation. At least from the date, other things would follow. If it doesn't work with Tom, there is Frank, Mark, Ken, Philip etc. Men are never limited in number.

One-time rejection should not scare you. It is not a death sentence. The person you are wooing can only say no. And this "no" can either be rude, polite or subtle. There is no terminal disease attached to it. You have to stop living in fear of the unknown. The fear of rejection is also the fear of the unknown. You don't know for sure, yet. You don't know if the answer will be no. If the answer is really no, why should it hurt you? Why should it hurt you that someone else exercised a right to choice and decision? The same way you made the choice of desiring that person and also making the request, so also does that person have the right to accept or decline. It is fair play. This understanding will take away that paralyzing fear that rejection invokes in people.

Periodic rejection

Rejection does not always happen once. When rejection happens once, it is easier to deal with it. You can get over it and move on (even if some people don't ever get over theirs) A periodic rejection is like peeling off the face of your wound occasionally. When it should have healed properly, something comes and opens it up. Perhaps, in this case, the problem is not with the rejection but the fact that the supposed victim hasn't discovered the antidote to rejection – which is understanding that rejection does not define you and that people will reject you because it is their right to do so. It has nothing to do with your self-worth.

One of the ways that rejection happens periodically, is when you get multiple "no" from the same person, because you keep asking and hoping that there would be a change of decision. There is a place of consistency, this is arguably true, but, adults are expected to know what they want. If an adult wants you to keep asking many times over before saying a yes, he/she clearly, isn't decisive enough.

Unlike the one-time rejection, periodic rejection can diminish your positive self-esteem faster. Imagine asking for the same thing, over and over again. It naturally would make a beggar out of you, especially if it is from the same person. It has a way of painting a very negative picture of you in your own eyes. You get to see yourself lesser than you should. Whether it is romance, finance-based, family rejection etc, it doesn't change the fact that it hurts when you have to receive the same negative response more than once from the same person.

Periodic rejection can take the form of a man who treats his wife with disrespect, every time she gets pregnant. Some men are like that. They are at their worst behavior whenever their wives are gestating. It is agreed that this action is a product of ignorance, which can be promoted by male superiority complex and foolishness about the place of a father in the life of his child(ren). Periodic rejection can also occur during times of illness or when there is loss of job.

Periodic rejection at your place of work could take the form of the employer acting up whenever it is time for pay. Some employers bring out their worst behaviors when it is time to pay salaries. This is finance-based rejection for the employee. It is a sad situation, where you receive insults in place of commendation for a job well done.

Continuous rejection

You can suffer consistent rejection if you are married or dating someone who is consistently disappointing you - Cheating on you, lying to you, treating you like trash. In fact this is the worst form of rejection that can leave very damaging effects on the victim.

The person rejecting you in this manner has no respect for you. He/she thinks so little about you and is not interested in giving you any form of respect. It is evident in both their words, actions and manner of actions towards you.

This mode of rejection increases the cycle of abuse in the society. The person who undergoes this form of abuse, internalizes it and becomes abusive towards other people. Most people wouldn't call this rejection, because they feel that rejection, is strictly an issue of saying no to someone's demands. This is not true. When you are married or dating somebody, there is a basic level of expectation you have for that person. You expect trust, care, fidelity, understanding, kindness, etc. If your partner fails to fulfill your expectation, it is rejection. For instance if a partner who is meant to love and respect you, decides to disrespect you; it is rejection.

There are two ways this mode of rejection occurs. Your partner might be the arrogant type who treats you like scum and doesn't care how you feel. He/she is overt in their acts of rejection towards you. This is the type that talks to you condescendingly, cheats on you flagrantly, is very hostile to you, does not give you room to make contributions, is very economical with kindness towards you etc.

There is also the covert form of continuous rejection. This type is carried out by very manipulative people. They craftily act like they care but in the long run, you end up experiencing the same rejection. They are like those uncles that would keep promising to help you until you become an octogenarian. They disguise their unwillingness to help you, under some disabilities and limitations. You might be busy sympathizing with them and thinking they are really making efforts to help you. Some so-called lovers are manipulatively so. They cheat on you while making it look like you caused it. They insult you and make it look like they have temper issues. They make promises without fulfilling any. You just keep hoping and expecting something that will never be. Sometimes it is only when they are through with you and ready to move on, that you will realize that you have actually gone through episodes of rejection.

Continuous mode of rejection, is responsible for the number of emotionally damaged individuals we have in the society. This is because most do not know what to do with rejection. They just give in and allow themselves to be damaged. This deals a very decisive blow on their self-esteem. Robs them of the will to seek the best out of life. They convince themselves that they are no good. Rejection can also enslave them to keep going in cycles of abuse where they unconsciously get attracted to people who would humiliate and treat them with disdain.

Living constantly in an atmosphere of rejection, can make the victim feel worthless. Most people who have been through rejection, usually lack confidence. You see them sticking to their comfort zones. They find it difficult reaching beyond their comfort zones to whatever they feel they truly deserve. They are most likely to settle for less. Since, it is better than being rejected. Who wants to receive a no for an answer? They just make do with whatever they can get without seeking too much. Only if you have seen a person paralyzed with the fear of rejection will you know how much effect rejection can have on people. In some cases when such people eventually walk out of those relationships or they are jilted, you see them being scared of relationships. They become suspicious of something as harmless as a compliment. Funny isn't it? They are the type you would call beautiful and they will rebuke you. If you offer them a relationship they are likely to say: "please leave me the way I am. I don't want trouble, before you will abandon me tomorrow." This shows to a large extent how they view themselves. For such people, it would require therapy for them to find themselves and rebuild the self-esteem they had lost. This is perhaps why it is imperative that you shouldn't stay long in abusive relationships, to the point where you internalize the abuse and make it yours.

CHAPTER FOUR

EXPECTATION

EXPECTATION

Rejection is always predicated by expectation. This is because you cannot be rejected if there was no expectation. Why do you feel bad after someone has said no to you? There, lies the basis of rejection. You are rejected when your expectations are not met. You have a need. You make a request. This request is accompanied by an expectation. You are hoping that your request will be granted. Or, you are hoping that your lover will always love you. You trust because you believe that you will not be disappointed. You go into marriage with expectations. You believe that your partner will keep the marriage vows you took together, but, you end up being disappointed, when he/she reneges on everything your marriage was built on.

You go for a job interview, believing that you will land the job, but, you end up losing out. You write a proposal for some money to finance your dreams, but, your potential benefactor does not oblige you. You expect that your parents will always look out for you but, finds out that they really don't care about you. All these are instances of rejection, and they all have accompanying expectations.

The best way to deal with this is to have neutrality of expectation. Don't be too confident in your expectation. Create room for probabilities. Some people allow themselves to develop high blood pressure over the possibility of a negative outcome of their expectations. This is very harmful to their mental and emotional being. They fail to realize that they don't have the power to decide for other people. You can only decide for yourself. If you are wise, you will know that the next person who holds the key to the fulfillment of your expectation, has the power to either say "yes" or "no". As such you will be helping yourself, by allowing your mind accommodate the possibility that it could be a no. When you do this, you are protecting yourself. Then, you ask yourself, what is the worst case scenario? The answer is "no" of course. What other harm can a no do to you? Nothing. If you fail to see it this way, you will be empowering that negative answer against yourself. You will not be able to focus your mind on alternatives. Sadly, some people spend their lives crying over spilled milk, when they could just easily purchase another - if only they knew.

The battle with ego limits your capacity to accept that your expectations didn't come through. Self-pity is actually powered by ego. Ego makes you feel you shouldn't be rejected. It blinds you to the reality that the person saying "no" to you is actually making use of a legitimate right, just as you have the right to ask. You feel entitled. It should be noted that the greater your sense of entitlement, the higher your vulnerability to rejection.

Legitimate Expectation

Rejection simply put, means being disappointed of your expectations from people or things. Your expectations may be legitimate or illegitimate.
 They are legitimate when you have a right to them. For instance a wife is entitled to love from her husband. This is legitimate expectation. If her husband fails her, that is rejection. Most of the vows taken before a marriage contract finally comes into existence are to the effect that both parties would love, care and respect each other.

This means that both parties to a marriage are within their legitimate rights, when they expect love, care and respect from their partner. A wife who demands accountability from her husband is not erring. A husband who demands same from his wife is also not in error. If a wife expects her husband to protect her interests, she is not out of order. It is sad that people suffer very devastating rejection within the matrimonial circle. Ordinarily, marriage should grant people a certain level of safety and certainty, but, this isn't so. People still renege on marriage vows.

Having unfettered rights to expect anything from somebody, means it is legitimate. The expectation of a child from his/her parents is legitimate. Why won't a child legitimately expect love from his/her parents? When you give birth to a child, you automatically come under an obligation to love and care for that child. You are forbidden from complaining. Remember a child does not come into the world by his/her own doing. Parents bring about the conception and birth of children. The least you can do for a child is to show him/her some love. Parental love is compulsory, though it is not a "given". We still have parents who fail in that regard. The point being made, therefore, is that a child has legitimate expectations when it comes to parental love. Parents on the other hand are not exempted from expecting love from their children, though, parents are to show that love first, since vulnerability starts with the child not the parent. The children are usually the ones to be primarily in need of love. Of course an infant is in a more vulnerable position than an adult. This is why the foundation must be laid by the parent and not the child. Unlike marriage where two adults come into it, on an equal footing, parent to child experience is different. In this case one person (the parent) must start up the process and the child will reciprocate when he/she can.

If you expect someone who has been a beneficiary of your own benevolence to help you in times of need, you are legitimately expectant. One good turn they say, deserves another. Kindness should give birth to kindness. Sadly, this may not be the case. You are bound to be rejected by that person you stuck out your neck for in time of need.

Siblings are entitled to love from one another. If you are expecting a sibling to show you love, it is a very legitimate expectation. However, the legitimacy of an expectation, doesn't mean that rejection cannot occur. In fact you are more likely to experience rejection from places where you have stakes. Siblings end up rejecting one another because they are sometimes blinded by selfish personal desires. We live in a society where siblings betray siblings for selfish gains. Perhaps, blood isn't always thicker than water. There are times that random friends would offer you more loyalty than your own blood.

Romantically, it is legitimate for a man/woman to ask the person of the opposite sex for romantic relationship. A person who asks the opposite sex out for a relationship is not in error, as long as they both have no romantic entanglements to other people. This has nothing to do with status. It is enough that you are both people of opposite sex. Anybody can see anybody and desire them. It is power of choice. There are cases where women, especially, get mad because a certain male asked them out. They become flummoxed that a guy they think is beneath them was confident enough to desire them. This is an erroneous assumption. The better looking you are, and higher your class, the greater the number of people who would desire you. People have eyes for good things. You have no right to get mad at people for desiring you. There is a limit to the rights we all possess. You cannot tell people what to desire and what not to. That's impossible. You only have the right to decline their requests, but, not to determine what their desires should be.

When an employer states needed qualification for job-seekers and you go there with the specified qualifications, you have every legitimacy to be expectant that you will land the job. Though, in practice this is hardly possible. One thing is to qualify, and other thing is to be chosen. The decision to employ you is the exclusive reserve of the employer. You don't have the right to compel an employer to employ you. Yes, we are aware that your qualification is everything that the employer needs, but, it is the final decision of the employer to decide if he/she wants you or not. We seem to miss the point –

which is that people still have rights to turn down good things. This is also true for the employee. You have a right to turn down a job offer, even if it comes with the best unprecedented terms and conditions. It is power of choice.

Illegitimate Expectation

There are expectations that violate the rights of other people and as such are regarded as illegitimate expectations. The illegitimacy is premised on the fact that your expectation, might be an infringement of another person's rights and position. It may not be the rights of the person whom you are directly requesting from. It may be the rights of another person, but that doesn't change the fact that it is illegitimate.

It is imperative that I address this because I see a lot of people demanding things they have no rights to and getting mad when they are declined. This is a product of entitlement mentality. The world does not revolve around you. If we must coexist happily and harmoniously, then we must be willing to recognize the limits of our rights and the extent of other people's rights. Most of the cases of murder, theft, arson and physical harm that are meted on unsuspecting victims, for saying no, wouldn't have occurred if only we understood that we are not meant to exceed our rights in pursuit of happiness and personal pleasures.

People get angry from illegitimate expectations and even go to the extent of harming other people. When they can't harm you, they would come up with emotional blackmail and begin to sound like you have hurt them. The reality is that you didn't hurt them by rejecting them. They are hurting themselves by failing to cooperate with reality.

 A job seeker who applies for a job with the right qualification will be right to have legitimate expectations of landing that job. This isn't the same for a job seeker who applies with a wrong qualification and expects a miracle to happen. People will not make heaven by a miracle. They will make heaven by doing what God expects them to do. I don't see Christians expecting God to bend his own standards for them, but they pray all the time to God to bend the standards of fellow humans for them. This sounds like fraud to me, but then, it is not the subject of discourse here, so, I will pass. When you are applying for a job, it is wisdom for you to pay attention to the job requirements. When they say come with B.Sc. Accounting, don't go there with a B.Sc. Sociology. Respect yourself!

When they say people with second class upper division should apply, don't apply with your third class. If you however, apply with a qualification other than what has been stipulated, understand that, you are doing that at your own peril. You have no legitimate expectation, because your application is already standing on a paralyzed leg. This also doesn't mean that it is impossible to land the job. What you should note is that your expectations are illegitimate. If you are rejected, you have no reason to be angry. You were wrong from the onset.

Though you didn't qualify for the job, there is still rejection if the job is not given to you. You must understand that it is their right to have rejected you. You left them no choice. It is simple. When you go to an eatery where they sell only

Amala and ewedu, if you are not a fan of such food, you will definitely walk away to another eatery where you will find the food that will appeal to you. You are within your rights when you do that. The food seller has no right to be mad at you. At each point in our lives, there is always an interplay of choices and desires. When this happens, somebody will lose, and another will win. Hence the saying: "we lose some, and win some."

As long as you have other people to deal with, you can't always have your way.

When you request that your lover gives you something that they can't afford, it is an illegitimate expectation. The keyword there is "affordability" not "willingness to give". How do you expect people to give you what they can't afford? Why don't you give it to yourself, if it were that easy? You can only get mad when you are convinced that he/she can afford what you ask for, but is unwilling to oblige you. Yet, your anger will not be necessary if you understand that they have a right to say no to you. The world will actually be a better place if we minimize our entitlement mentality.

Is it legitimate to request that a man or woman entangled with another person, becomes romantically involved with you? No. You have the right to ask. Once they admit that they are involved with someone else, the wise thing for you to do is to let them go. But, some people have chosen to cause unnecessary pains to themselves and others. This is why you will see a man getting mad at a married woman who has refused to date him. Here in Nigeria, a lot of foolish men heckle and bully other mens' wives into romantic relationships with them. They could use job security, money or some other machinations to trap them.

I am not ignorant that a married woman is an adult and has the sole right to date another man other than her husband, if she wants. The worst thing that could happen is that she would get a divorce when caught or when she is tired of being fraudulent. However, this must be of her own doing. She must go into such relationship without being under duress, force or fraud. It is something that should naturally occur as an exercise of her personal right to choice.

What I consider a problem, is when she says an emphatic no, yet, the man wooing her wouldn't bulge. There has been cases of men who threatened married women with losing their jobs, if they refused to date them. This is a case of entitlement mentality gone wild. How can we maintain world peace when people, do not understand the meaning of the word "boundary"? If you must go out and have an affair, why don't you seek ladies who are single and without romantic attachments to anybody. Your expectation with them will be very legitimate. How do you feel when your wife or husband is under threat by someone desiring to date him/her?

If we all go on to attempt to date other people's spouses forcibly, what would our world turn into? What legacy are we leaving for the next generation? Does it make us appear responsible, regardless of our level of scholarship and exposure? When you threaten people into giving in to your selfish inordinate passions and desires, you reveal yourself as a person without class. Your status in the society becomes inconsequential. A person with class will understand not to impose personal desires on other people. I bet nobody taught you this. It is okay to desire somebody's wife or husband. It is okay to ask them out, if you can't avoid it. It is also okay to let them go if they are not interested in what you want. It shows you know your worth.

Well, not all cases of illegitimate expectations come with threats or force. Some come with emotional blackmail. We could easily overlook somebody claiming that he would die if a single lady does not accept his romantic overtures. But, how do we handle a married man who is making romantic advances towards a married woman and claiming that he would die if she says no? It is either he is ignorant of what the word boundary means and therefore has allowed his negative self-esteem to lead him on (though I find this hard to believe, since he is likely not to allow his own wife oblige her male "toasters") or he is just a manipulative character seeking to take advantage of vulnerable and gullible women. Whichever the case may be, it still doesn't speak positively. It is all shades of infringement of human rights and violation of self dignity.

As I already stated above, it is okay for you to woo a man or woman that has been spoken for, but becomes a problem when you are determined to have your way despite knowing that such person is already attached to someone else. That's a level of selfishness, potent enough to start World War III. This person is not interested in the welfare of the person he/she is wooing. He is only concerned with how to satisfy his/her personal interests, even at the detriment of the other person. They come with lies like: "I can't do without you". Yet, this same person has a partner at home that they actually avowed their love, loyalty and fidelity to.

The point being that their expectation is illegitimate. They have no right to the thing they desire. Even if they have a right to desire, to desire is one thing, to have is another. It is like the biblical story of Moses on mount Nebo, where God told him, that he could see the promise land but entering into it would be impossible. Everyday when we walk on the street and encounter people. We admire people, we desire them. This is okay. It is harmless, since it is still at the realm of our minds. The eyes is meant to see and appreciate things that appeals to it. This is why you see a married man staring at another lady who appeals to his sight. It is permissible. What is not permissible is when you decide to take that desire, a step forward by trying to acquire what you have admired. This is because people will definitely get hurt.

It is simple. You go to a bank. You see somebody holding a very large amount of cash. You desire it. It is okay. You can increase your hustle, if you are not earning that much at that time. That sight could be a motivation for you to work harder and smarter. It only becomes a problem when you decide to acquire that money belonging to the other person, by stealing it outrightly or defrauding that person.

If you request for something that you have no legitimate right to, you can as well be wise enough not to feel entitled about it. When your expectation is illegitimate, it is safer to allow things to take their natural route without trying to bully people into granting your requests. If they must oblige you, let them do it on their own terms and volition. Don't set yourself up for pains and emotional disaster. Don't hurt yourself intentionally.

POLITE NO

People say "no" to one another each day. It is a very common occurrence. We say no at home, church, mosque, market, school, workplace, in relationships etc. Every rejection experience is premised on the word or action, "No".

You can be lucky to be rejected in a polite way, where you have to deal with only the rejection and not the manner of rejection. From experience, I have found that what hurts people is not just the rejection, but also the manner of the rejection.

I have wooed some ladies in my life who rejected me in a very polite way. Prominent amongst them, is a certain lady I wooed in the year 2015. After asking her out, she told me to give her some days to get back to me, since she had something on her hands. I agreed and gave her time. When, she got back to me, she said: "Victor, you are a very great guy. You are the kind of man a woman would naturally pray for. But, right now, I am not emotionally prepared to handle a relationship. I still have issues that I am dealing with. Please bear with me."

I listened to her as she explained her stance politely. My respect for her increased greatly. There are ladies like this, who have mastered the act of being polite. She even took her politeness a step forward by explaining why she wouldn't be able to oblige my request. All she needed to do was to tell me that she wasn't available for a relationship. That was all. There is no way I would have felt offended by her, considering the manner in which she made her position known to me.

I have been wooed by ladies too. In each case I politely turned down the offer without being rude and making the lady feel less than a human. The truth is that being wooed by a person does not mean you are superior or a better man. It is simple. That person is interested in you. I will also like to add, that not everybody who woos you, has your interest at heart. This is probably where some women get it wrong. They believe that a man that woos you genuinely cares about you. I have even seen women who play tough or what we call "hard to get". In their understanding they believe that a man that puts up with your hard-to-get stunts truly loves you. Strangely, they don't know that some men put up with your hard-to-get madness because they want to have the last laugh. These are the type of men who are likely to treat you with scorn eventually. We must understand that relationship, is a two-way traffic. You are not doing anybody a favour by dating or marrying them. Having this understanding will prevent you from making things too difficult for those who are interested in you.

Being polite to those who make requests from you, reveals how healthy your self-esteem is and that you are a person of class. You can agree with me that the manner of the response is usually based on the personality and intelligence of the person being wooed.

However, a polite "no" is not only practicable in

romance related issues. Even when you are making a financial request, you can still receive a polite response, albeit unfavorable. An employer turning down your request for a job, can still say it politely, without making you feel worthless. There are people who are so polite, that they would add "please" or "I am sorry" to whatever negative response they give to you.

In the course of a marriage or romantic relationship, a partner can decide to walk away without provocation. People get tired of a relationship, not always because the partner did anything to hurt them. Some might be because they entered into those relationships with the wrong expectations or wrong mindset. People evolve daily. At the point when they realize that they can no longer feel fulfilled in that relationship, you see them, seeking ways to walk away. This is true about some women who walk out of marriages without being offended. There are men too who do the same. The injured partner might start thinking that he/she has done anything wrong but in reality they did nothing.

You can be lucky to have a partner who is humane and reasonable. This is the partner that will be polite while taking the steps of rejection. This partner is likely to have a talk with you and explain politely why he/she is walking out of the relationship. It doesn't in anyway minimize the effect of the rejection. It only shows that you are dealing with a partner who has an active conscience and who is willing to do things respectfully.

In some job positions, the employer could decide to relieve an employee of his/her job. This employer would do so, in a very polite manner, without putting the employee through the harrowing experience of a rude rejection. Sometimes certain payments and even prior notice could be given to the victim to make the rejection easy to bear.

RUDE NO

This is the greatest fear of most people, when it comes to rejection. We have a palpable fear of receiving a rude no for an answer. There was a time I had that fear. We are always scared of the humiliation that comes with it.

The truth is that people who are rude with their negative answers, are most times people of very negative self-esteem. You don't expect them to behave better than their self-esteem. They often think that there will be no tomorrow for you. When they reject you, they do it with arrogance, such that you would be tempted to think that your life has ended.

Their actions can force you to seek alternatives and live your life proving a point. The psychological effect of a rude no, is that you tend to think less of yourself. There is every possibility that you would start looking down on yourself. Some people don't ever heal from that experience, especially in the absence of an emotional healer, to assist them.

I see quite a number of people suffering from the after-effects of the rejection they suffered years back. Some have been told that they are useless and can never amount to anything. This is so gross. How can you, in addition to rejecting a person, tell them that they cannot amount to anything? Who does that? Can you see beyond your today? The only thing in life that is very constant is change. Nobody is entirely predictable.

When you ask for something from some people, be it a relationship, or money or job or some other forms of assistance, there are people that will tell you no in a very rude manner that you end up depressed. Most times it is not just the rejection that would bring about the depression but the manner in which you were rejected. It could also occur at a point in the existence of a relationship – whether romantic, marriage, financial, career, job etc. For instance some people break up with their lovers after a while in their relationship. Let's take an example. A husband and wife have been living happily since the first day of their marriage. After about ten years of that marriage, the woman having had three children, physical features altered a bit and she no longer looks like what she looked like in the early days of their marriage. Her husband will suddenly fall into midlife crisis and no longer feel attracted to her. This is usually as a result of being obsessed with looks rather than personality.

While it is not wrong to have certain specs for looks, I think it is wrong to give up on someone who has been there for you, and whose new look has been occasioned by sacrifices made for the common good.

He suddenly starts getting attracted to another woman. Then he wakes up one day and breaks up with his wife. He goes on to tell her how she is no longer attractive, how he can't deal any longer, how she should get the hell out of his life. He doesn't consider the impact of those words, but he goes on to say them, after all. A woman who has been his partner for ten years and more suddenly experiences not just rejection but a rejection that is very rude in nature. This experience shatters people especially because they have been trained to believe that marriage is a safe zone. What they failed to realize is that marriage vows are made by people and since people are unpredictable, we cannot say for sure how long they would stick to their vows.

In my experience as an Emotional Doctor, I have dealt with people of different categories of emotional hurt. I have healed women who came out from abusive marriages – most of them battered and disgruntled and disillusioned with life. It didn't take me long to heal them and show them that life is still beautiful. I had to take them through series of therapy to open up their minds to the concept of self-love in its totality. I helped them to find themselves and develop the desire to live again. I have cases where the estranged and prodigal husband tried coming back into their lives after seeing that they moved on to enjoy the beauty of life. These are people who could have become suicidal and even lost their lives. I was able to touch them and give them reasons to stay alive.

In the game of love, we often assume that things would remain the way they are forever. So, we place blind faith on something we aren't sure of. This is why people wake up to find that rejection has come upon them like hurricane. In my book-Emotional Insurance, I outlined ways you can prepare your mind and heart to love without getting hurt in the process and all of those ways are without side effects. Love is a beautiful thing, when you understand how to love.

There is a man I know who was with the late Nigerian musician OJB, the day Ayo Balogun, popularly known as Wizkid, came to him and requested for assistance in his musical career. OJB listened to the songs and immediately told Wizkid that he should get out of his office, that his songs were whack and wouldn't make a success out of him. Wizkid walked away in tears. After a while Banky W took Wizkid and gave him his support. The end result is the successful star musician we have today as Wizkid. This is a typical example of a rude no. I could go on narrating stories of other people's rejection experiences. However, I would prefer, you think through and recall all your own experiences. At this moment it is about you. Therefore your own story is paramount. I am dealing with you.

Not everybody will reject you in a polite manner. Many will be rude about it. If you didn't know this, you should know it and get used to it. You need to understand that the rudeness of the rejection, does not define you. It only shows the character of the person rejecting you not you. This is because another person can be put in that position and he/she will not be rude to you.

Same situation, different approaches. It reveals the personality of the person involved. Rejection is a human reality. The manner and way it occurs is dependent on the peculiarity of the individual carrying out the rejection.

I had a break-up (not heartbreak) at some point in my life's emotional voyage. Something happened and she got mad at me. I am not at liberty to give full details, especially since that is not the focus here. We were together the week before the incident. Everything was fine, that you could hardly predict that we would break-up the next week.

So, something happened. She didn't ask me for explanation. Never gave me a chance to at least defend myself. It had nothing to do with infidelity, by the way. The time she could have given me to defend myself, she spent it abusing and raining generational insults on me. In conclusion, she told me that it was over between us. It sounded like a joke. I kept pleading with her to hear me out. The truth of the matter is that she misinterpreted a situation, of which I should blame her for not being meticulous with details.

She told me to get the hell out of her life and called me names that some people might regard as unprintable. We were having this exchange on the phone. So, I decided to go see her and perhaps woo her to hear me out. I got there and when I knocked she opened.

"What do you want?" She screamed, almost bursting my ear drums.
 "I want us to talk, please."

"I'm sorry but there is nothing to talk about."

"Baby! Please hear me out", I said.

Her next words hit me like sledgehammer on my chest.
"You are useless to me, I don't want you occupying space in my life."

She wasn't sounding like the woman I was with the previous week. What hurt me was not that she was breaking up. Anybody has the inalienable right to walk out of any relationship. It is your right. And this right is not limited by reason that the partner you want to leave is treating you well. People still turn down good things or don't they? So, you can choose to walk out of a relationship, even if your partner is treating you well.

What hurt me was the way she was talking and treating me condescendingly. I am very reasonable. You want out, I would oblige you. That's how developed my mind is. The fact that she was insulting me and humiliating me all in the process of breakup was my major pain.

I accepted to leave, but asked for two minutes of her time. She gave me audience. Then, I told her that break-up should never be done in a demeaning and humiliating way. Unless you are walking out of, say: domestic violence, chronic infidelity or some other vices. But, a situation where there is no vice but just a disagreement and you really wish to break-up, be reasonable enough to be polite in your approach. It does not make you any less than you are. It rather earns you respect.

She stood there looking at me in silence as I

explained. I told her that one of the reasons people become vengeful after break-up is usually the manner of the break-up. You see them trying to harm you just to redeem their bruised ego.

Even as you break-up, don't forget that you are dealing with a human. Don't make them feel worthless. As for me I didn't have that problem. My self-esteem was not at risk, but then, not everybody is like me. There are some people who will never be able to handle it the way I did. After educating her, I thanked her for her time and went back home.

It wasn't up to a month before my vindication came and she reached out to me seeking reconciliation. We did reconcile but never came back as partners. Reason being, I saw how much value she attached to me, through her words.

Don't treat people like lepers because you want out of a relationship. It is your right to leave but don't abuse it by doing it the wrong way. We know that there are people who will still be vengeful regardless of how you break-up with them, but you have to play your part well.

SUBTLE NO

This manner of rejection, appears harmless but it does harm the victim as much as other manners of rejection. There are people who will not say no to you, either politely or rudely. These people are those who would subtly say no to you and keep you in slavery for a long while, until you are able to get smart and find your way out.

Two reasons that can lead to this is when the person is unwilling to make you feel bad. So they keep postponing the evil day and hoping that someday you might be able to pull the trigger, yourself. Another reason is when they have something to gain from you, so, they pretend to be with you. They can neither say a rude or polite no. They just say it through their actions. Some days they are nice to you, other days they are at their worst behavior. They are passing the message that they detest you, but, you definitely won't see it. You are obviously blinded by love as it were, that you would interpret it as mood swings. But, do you know that mood swings should make that person to be shitty towards him/herself? They don't have to transfer it to you. In fact, if they truly care about you, your presence should help their mood.

You ask a woman out and she knows that she isn't into you but because there is something she thinks she can gain from you, she would play along. Often, it is usually about money and material things. They won't say no to you. They will just keep you there to service a particular need in their life. They give you a false sense of security and you end up believing that you are in safe hands.

The one way you will find out, is that their attitude towards you will be that of someone extending some privileges to you. They would talk to you disrespectfully and condescendingly. Every time, they would look for ways to belittle you and make you depend on them for validation, despite that you are the one sponsoring your own misery. The signs are always there.

Some men lack the integrity to say a direct no to you, whether politely or rudely. They would rather string you till infinity. Whenever you demand for better treatment, they will quickly remind you that you were the one who wooed them. I bet they believe that there is something special about being wooed by a woman and as such their self-esteem finds some sort of satisfaction from being able to rub it on your face. Truth is, anybody can woo anybody. Being the person who initiates a relationship, doesn't reduce your worth. Just as being told no, doesn't also reduce your worth. The earlier we changed these narratives, the better. We have succeeded in enslaving people mentally with our skewed narratives of how relationships should come into existence.

You will see this class of men living off women financially and sexually. They won't tell you no. They would just keep you there and treat you consistently like trash until you are able to find the will to walk away. This subtle "no" can damage a person's psyche and self-esteem. It will tell you that you are no good and that you don't deserve any better. Some people in such relationships don't bother thinking of leaving because they believe no one else would desire them. They define their lives on the treatment they receive from such abusive partners.

Another way that people reject you subtly is by holding you captive with promises. There are people that will keep you close, by promising you things they won't fulfill. You will keep hoping that one day they will fulfill their promises to you. The reality is that they have no such intentions. They are actually believing that you will become smarter and find your way after realizing that it is all a charade. Sadly, some people never get to break that influence over their lives. They will follow to the end. People who reject people in this manner are cowards. They can't come clean and say no. Instead, they would keep giving you false hope that something good will come out of your relationship with them.

Sometimes when you eventually decide to find your way out, you will end up doubting yourself and feeling like you are making a huge mistake. This is how you know that you have internalized the abuse from that experience. You should be able to know when somebody has no plans of fulfilling their promise to you, then walk. You will not die.

CHAPTER FIVE

PECULIARITIES OF REJECTION

PECULIARITIES OF REJECTION

Rejection is a life-time experience.

People will always reject you and you will always reject people in different areas of your life. There is no end to it. It is part of our human experience, because our values, choices, desires and interests won't always be the same.

So, instead of thinking how to avoid rejection, we would focus on how to deal with it when it occurs. You can't avoid rejection. You can rather learn what it is and get used to it.

Most people who tremble at the mention of rejection do that because they don't know that rejection is part of our daily existence. They also are probably not attentive enough to see that they also reject other people. It is a cycle. Sometimes you can't afford not to reject people. For instance, if you like to date fair skin people, you are naturally going to reject dark skin people. It is not because you hate them or anything it's just that they are not what you want. Just like the way we reject food. I am an Igbo person from Nigeria. My people enjoy eating "ukwa" which is breadfruit. There is nothing you would do to me to make me desire that food. People look at me strangely, when I say I don't like eating it. Does it mean that ukwa is bad, no. People who have more name than I have, eat ukwa. It is what it is. Choice. I don't like it. This is what it looks like when we make choices. If a lady decides not to date a guy who is not lettered, there should be no hard feelings. It is choice. It also shouldn't make the guy feel little about himself.

We all want what we want. It is a reality that we cannot escape from. The best you can do is understand how not to allow it break you down.

You must always anticipate rejection.

It is not negative expectation. It is protection. When you anticipate it, you won't be shocked if it comes. You must always know that anybody can fail you, regardless of the person's relationship with you. Nobody deserves absolute trust. When you make a request from anybody, whether it is financial, romantic, career-related etc, always remember that your request can be declined. This should protect you from harming yourself when the rejection occurs. Always anticipate that the answer can be no. It is foolishness to assume that you will always get yes for an answer. Some people believe so much in their personal charm that they don't ever imagine that anybody can say no to them.

You should know that the typical answer to every request, is either "yes", "no" or "wait". You can't make the request and also give the answer. This shows that you cannot determine the answer yourself. That aspect is the exclusive reserve of the person to whom the request is directed.

Rejection reveals the power of choice

When people reject you, they are making a legitimate use of their power of choice.

It might be deceptive or honest but the point is that they are using their right. They have the right to choose you or not. Having this knowledge would help you get over rejection when it occurs.

It also means you have the same right to reject other people. No matter how good and well-meaning you are as a person, people are also going to suffer rejection in your own hands. Getting mad when you are rejected is like saying nobody should have the power to make choices.

The word choice reveals that something is definitely going to be preferred above another. That is why that word "choice" exists in our language. For you to make a choice, it means there must be rejection. Wherever there is choice there must be rejection. Taking away rejection means we must also take away choice.

Unfortunately, the choice isn't just about things and inanimate objects. It affects humans. There is a reason people say: "have you made a choice of a life partner?" It shows that you must choose out of the majority. You must choose the person you want. When you carry out that activity of making choice, you will inadvertently reject someone else. That is how we maintain balance in the world.

Somebody must be rejected for another person

to be accepted. If A rejects you, B will accept you. Like the example I gave, they often say that one man's meat is another man's poison. The person rejected by one person, becomes the best choice of another. That is how life is. We must get used to this. Rejection exists because choice exists. Take one away and automatically destroy the other.

You can't stop anybody from rejecting you.

That aspect of their lives is strictly theirs to decide. You can only control your own actions but not that of others. Yes, you can influence how people treat you, but you can't decide how they would treat you.

People allow the fear of rejection to make them do unimaginable things. They go to the extent of making illegitimate sacrifices in their bid to preempt rejection. What they fail to realize is that you really can't stop anybody from rejecting you. Rejection is a product of the power of choice and we all have it.

Outside the desire to abuse and control people, another reason that people cast love spells on others is because they don't want to experience rejection. The fear of taking no for an answer, makes people go to the extent of trying to use supernatural methods to compel love. It should be noted that any love founded on spells is not true love. True love means you would also allow the person to make his/her choice. You can't claim to love somebody and take away their power of choice. I know you love him/her, but you really have to allow them make their choice. You should let them decide if they also want you. Love is only love when it is based on mutualism. One-sided love is not love.

Rejection doesn't mean you are not good enough

Some people reject you because they think you are too good for them, yet you go on to torture yourself with self-pity.

This is perhaps, one of the ironies of rejection.

There are people who can see you for who you are. They actually believe you to be way above their league. In order not to cause pain for themselves, you see them rejecting you. They aren't doing that to spite you. They are being protective of themselves.

There are times when you have very poor opinion about yourself, then you go woo someone who sees you from an esteemed perspective. This person might turn you down, not because they think you are not good enough. In reality, they just think they are not good enough for you and they turn you down. You are actually the person who is too good for them. Unfortunately, because you can't see yourself for the person you really are, you might end up thinking you weren't good enough. This could further damage your self-esteem. You will wallow in self-pity and bemoan your rejection.

Some people who have attained certain levels of stardom have been known to say negative things about those who rejected them when they were still in obscurity. The truth of it all is that some of the people who rejected them, already saw their future and felt they won't be able to fit into their lives in the future. In other to prevent the pains that will come in the future, they decided to reject them. A person can reject you because he/she thinks you deserve a better person. The right thing for you is not to go on and whine about the rejection. Except in rare cases, the person rejecting you may not explain to you why he/she rejected you. Only some, will be confident enough to tell you that they consider you too good for them. So, before you start thinking you were not good enough, pause and imagine that it could be the other way round. It could be you who is too good for the other person.

That person might be trying to save you from regrets. The regrets that comes when you step into the reality of the life you were meant to live.

Nothing is a given except it is 100% under your control.

You can be qualified, classy, wealthy, good looking and yet, suffer rejection. It is not under your control. This is something you should know and accept, if you want to have peace in life.

Our desires and interest are never the same. Don't ever imagine that the next person wants what you want. I have seen beautiful, independent and amazing ladies who are single. Some really want to be married but haven't got the suitors they want. In our society, people are quick to add that there must be something wrong with such people – apparently, they have bad character. This is a very foolish assumption.

Marriage and relationship is a different issue all together. A woman doesn't marry herself. That a woman who is supposedly complete with all qualities, is single, doesn't mean something is wrong with her. She won't woo herself. And even when she woos a man, he has to accept. She has no control over who will accept her. She can only decide who she wants. The most frustrated women I have seen are those who tried to buy the love of men with money. You can't make someone want you. You can make yourself desirable but the final acceptance is still a decision to be made by that person.

Having a very good academic degree doesn't mean you must land that job. You have no control over it. You could have helped somebody in the past and now you need their help. There is no guarantee that you will get that help. People should know these things, so they can minimize the pain that comes with rejection.

No matter how good you are, somebody is definitely going to reject you; and no matter how bad you are, somebody will accept you. It is life. We don't control people's choices. It is more about who they are than who we are. Quit trying to control people's desires. Allow them to make their choices.

Rejection does not reduce your worth

The mistake people make after rejection is to think that they are worthless. They end up being sorrowful and feeling sorry for themselves. It affects their self-esteem in no positive way.

They fail to realize that rejection, in reality does not reduce your worth. You are still who you are. Rejection only means you are not their best choice. Must you be everybody's choice? Hell no! Just like you don't desire everybody you meet, other people are also entitled to that level of freedom to make choices. It does not in any way suggest a reduction in worth.

No, is the word. It is simple. I don't want you. Nothing else. You keep your head high and walk away from rejection. You should also know that other people survive after you have rejected them. If truly rejection reduces your worth, then people will not be able to make progress after rejection. As an individual, there is no rejection that bothers me, there was a time I was scared of rejection. A time when rejection held me captive. Not anymore. I know my worth. I also know that I cannot be good for everybody. What matters is that I am good for myself. Every other person is at liberty to decide if they want me or not.

I have been wooed by ladies who eventually turned into enemies because I turned down their offers. I wish I was able to help them see that rejecting them didn't reduce their worth. Women tend to struggle so much with rejection. It affects the way they look at themselves. It could make them think they are ugly. They fail to understand that not everybody would desire the most beautiful girl. The former beauty Queen, Agbani Darego, is a very beautiful lady. There was a time I told a friend that I can't date Agbani. She is not my spec. Yet, we all know she is a beautiful lady. Men who are above me in class and achievement, worship at her feet. It will be foolish to assume that because I don't fancy her, therefore, she isn't good enough.

The fact remains that we will make choices in life and those choices won't favour everybody. If somebody's choices doesn't favour you, it has nothing to do with your worth. Only you can determine your worth. It is not in the power of anybody to do that for you. Your validation lies in your hands.

Don't live your life proving points to those who rejected you.

There are so many people who do not recover from rejection. Even when they move on to live their lives, they still unconsciously enslave themselves to those who rejected them. They allow themselves to psychologically depend on those people for validation.

This is a very frustrating life to live. The only person you need to prove points to, is yourself. Those people who rejected you, don't care. They aren't bothered with whatever you want to become.

You will see a woman who rejected a man because he had no money. This man will immediately start working on his dreams. In the process, another lady will become interested in him and love him wholeheartedly. She will give her all to see that he becomes the man he wants to be. In his own mind, all that matters to him is to become something so he can brag about his success to that lady that rejected him, and probably win her love. He wouldn't bother much about the lady that is making sacrifices for him because he is still trapped in the past.

When he eventually becomes successful, he will run after that lady that rejected him. In some cases, if she is still available she will give him a chance. This will gladden his heart so much. In his ignorance, he wouldn't know that she actually cares only for what she can get out of him. He will begin to treat the lady that stood by him, like trash. He will demean her and make her life miserable, in his bid to please the other lady. After he has lost the lady who loved him, he will start up a relationship with the other lady. The other lady will be with him until he has lost almost everything he achieved and back to his previous condition. It is only at that point that she will leave him a second time. You will see him reaching out to the lady he rejected and trying to solicit for her support again. One thing is noticeable. The lady he was obsessed with didn't add any value to him. People only add value to you when they care about you.

The problem here, is that he refused to move on. He might have moved on physically but emotionally he was still enslaved. All he was fighting for was to win the love of that other lady. There are a lot of people living this kind of life today. They are doing things and making efforts to impress those who rejected them. There is no need for such unproductive life. When people reject you, let them go. Move on. You don't owe them any explanation. Even if you end up a failure it does not change anything. Your success doesn't matter to them. Live your life for you and not for people who rejected you. Don't enslave yourself. You have no need to prove any point to them. Trying to prove a point to them will put you under pressure. If you want to live a life that is enjoyable, then avoid trying to impress people. They are not that important. The most important person in your life is you. Strive to be better than where you are today. People who rejected you don't deserve to have such influence over your life. They don't.

CHAPTER SIX

I AM NOT DEAD YET

I AM NOT DEAD YET

Except in peculiar situations, most people who reject you always don't expect that you will survive the experience. For them it is a death sentence. Death here may not necessarily mean death in the true sense, but "end". They believe within them that you cannot transcend that situation. Thus, there is a certain sense of indifference or nonchalance that accompanies their actions of rejection – they care little about how you will feel or what that experience might bring about in your life.

The only person who knows at that moment, that you are not dead, is you. You hold that knowledge and it is a very precious knowledge. It is precious because that is the foundation on which you are going to build your "rise" or restoration. A dead person is dead and gone. If people and situations can convince you that you are dead, then you are dead and nothing can be done about your situation.

The dead do not talk, nor walk. This explains why the knowledge that you are still alive is priceless.

It simply means all is not over for you. Those who rejected you might think it is over for you but no, the final power resides with you. Make a 'comeback'.

Despite the seeming hopelessness of any situation, the knowledge that you are still alive is more than enough lifeline. It is a last resort. You just have to hold on to it like someone down a deep pit and holding unto a rope, with which he/she is trying to climb out of that pit.

Just like a rope of survival, is not going to save you independently of your own efforts, so also the knowledge that you are alive cannot save you unless you use it positively. You are going to make conscious effort. Knowledge alone is not enough. You must add action to your knowledge in order to make it productive. You can have all the knowledge in the world but failure to add action to your knowledge will make that knowledge unproductive.

Knowing that you are not dead is not enough. You have to prove it, both to yourself and those who gave up on you. You must stand up from where you are and make your next move. Those who failed or disappointed you will not expect you to rise again. You have to disappoint them. There are people who think that without them you will never amount to anything, disappoint them.

Make up your mind to make a meaning out of your life, despite the rejection you have faced. That thing they refused you, go out there and find it without their support. If you were denied love, happiness, Job, etc, go out there and find it. Let them know that their rejection didn't kill you. It only killed your hope in them – which is not a bad thing in itself. Your hope shouldn't be on anybody. People will fail you.

Stand before your mirror, look into your eyes and tell yourself that you are not dead. This is not some random positive self-talk affair. You are not saying it just to feel good. Some people say nice things to themselves without meaning what they say. It will not be useful to them. If you must say something to yourself, you must believe in it.

So, when you stand before that mirror don't just

say things because you are privileged to have an organ of speech, say them because you know they are true. Tell yourself that you are alive and believe in it.

That feeling of hopelessness after an episode of rejection, should not be your lot. You are still alive. That is all you need, to find your way. The knowledge that you are alive and not dead, would serve as a pedestal for your next line of action. Everything you will do after your rejection experience would be premised on the fact that you are not dead or permanently hopeless.

When you are not dead but in a situation or location that could easily pass you off as dead, something is expected. You are expected to make a move. You don't just sit there and be buried alongside the dead. You must do something to show that you are alive. It is not enough to know or be convinced that you are 'living,' you have to show it in your actions. Stand up. Plan. Do something, anything, but don't just sit at the site of your rejection. Walk.

CHAPTER SEVEN

IT MADE ME STRONGER

IT MADE ME STRONGER

"What doesn't kill you makes you stronger."
This statement reveals profound truth that the undiscerning might not comprehend.

If something does not kill you, it makes you stronger. This however is not an absolute truth. Some people survive near death experiences and become "vegetables" for the rest of their lives – that doesn't look like "a stronger version" to me.

What is left unsaid is that how you react to what happens to you will determine whether it will leave you weaker or stronger. It is all in the mind. Some People go through life challenges and come out stronger. They choose to see the bright side and hold on to it. The side you see is dependent on your organ of sight and its functionality. If you are always seeing negatives, then there is no hope for you.

Our approach to situation is more powerful than the situations themselves. So, what doesn't kill you makes you stronger, only if, you know how to convert it to strength. There are women who faced rejection at some point in their lives, instead of resigning to whatever is left of that situations they chose to turn their lives around, dramatically.

What makes one a survivor? There are people who call themselves survivors but that is just a verbal cliché. They are no survivors because they really didn't survive from the experience they claim to have survived from.

You are not a survivor if all your life is still regulated and controlled by the same experience you claim to have survived from. If your views and sentiments are largely influenced by that traumatic experience you had, you really haven't survived. Survival is much more than escaping partly hurt from danger. Perhaps, we tend to see survival, only from the physical perspective. We don't take into consideration, the psychological angle.

Very many people really don't survive. Their lives get altered and they spend their whole lives as shadows of their former selves. This doesn't look like survival to me. You will know that you have survived when that experience no longer has a negative effect on you. This does not happen in isolation. You have to make effort to let it go. When you let the experience go, you are setting yourself free. Dwelling in anger and hate towards those that rejected you is not a sign of survival, it is a sign of slavery and it hurts you, not them. As long as you are angry with them, you will never be free and happy. You will always think they hold the key to your life. In reality, nobody has such power over your life, except you hand them that power.

CHAPTER EIGHT

ENERGY CONVERSION

ENERGY CONVERSION

Rejection comes with or evokes very negative energy. This energy brings about despair, hopelessness, self-pity, bitterness etc, and it saps you of the will to do anything else that would better your life.

You feel drained, without any drive left within you to pursue after other options. The natural thing to do after rejection is to lose faith in yourself. You find yourself at that point where you think you are worthless. The longer you think about it the farther you step into the dungeon of hopelessness and bleakness.

Have you ever experienced rejection? Take a moment and imagine how you felt. You felt like your whole world had crashed – leaving you nothing else to live for. This same feeling is capable of damaging your self-esteem. There is so much harm that rejection does to us. It can alter the way we see ourselves and if nothing is done to remedy it, we might live for the rest of our lives feeling inadequate and almost useless to humanity.

The energy that comes with rejection, is not necessarily a weak one. It is strong and fast-acting. Do not be deceived to feel that because it drains you, that means it is a weak energy. Nothing could be farther from the truth. That energy is powerful and can be seen from its effect on you, the victim.

Having come to terms with the fact that you have been rejected, you shouldn't enable that negative energy in its effort to drain and leave you totally incapacitated. This is the point where you have to do some energy conversion. The duty on you is to convert that energy from negative energy to positive energy. It is in the best of your interest to do this, having in mind that it is the only way out of your situation. This is not the time to stay put and feel hopeless and powerless. You've got to do something that would transform your present situation.

Converting that negative energy to positive energy is about the simplest thing to do. A lot of people dwell so much on negativity. Ignorantly, they fuel their weaknesses by giving so much relevance to the negative thoughts that cloud their minds. What you empower in your mind, gives your life direction.

To convert your negative energy to positive energy, you have to see the bright side of your experience. No one else should do that for you. Every negative situation, has a positive side. It behooves you to discover the positive side of that rejection and focus on it. Instead of a negative energy that drains and keeps you down, you can convert it to positive energy that would motivate you to rise.

Avoid having a victim's mentality always. Victims are weak and consistently in need of help. They whine and whinge about their situation. Because they want to be pitied, they hardly ever try to muster courage and do something about their situation. They would rather sit there and complain to every ear that offers them the luxury of attentiveness. Ironically, the amount of time and energy it takes them to complain could have been spent in finding solution.

A victim will always be down. A victim will always

need help. A victim always want to maintain the status quo of his/her unfortunate situation. He/she will not attempt to take the bull by head. No. They are constantly in need of a savior. When they are not seeking a savior, they are crying and pitying themselves to oblivion. They allow their minds to be clouded with negativity and all that thoughts of helplessness. In such state, you will end up empowering your negative energy to keep you in perpetual powerlessness. You won't be motivated enough to rise from your ashes.

It is agreed that rejection is a terrible experience but you have the ultimate power to decide how things turn out. Should we all die or lose the drive to make a meaning of our lives, because of rejection? There has to be life after rejection – a life worth living. It is in your power to create a worthy life for yourself. You shouldn't put an end to your happiness because of an episode or more, of rejection. At the end of rejection, there should commence, another phase of your life. Each rejection should mark the end of a chapter in the book of your life. So, start over another chapter and make it worthwhile.

CHAPTER NINE

PLANTS GROW AT NIGHT

PLANTS GROW AT NIGHT

In 2008, SciencDaily.com revealed that tall spindly plants are a byproduct of "Shade Avoidance Syndrome," a scientific term for a plant's tendency to increase its production of the growth hormone auxin, allowing the plant to grow and stretch more rapidly toward sunlight and to improve its conditions.

Some other plants known as shade loving plants have learnt to adapt to their own situations. These group of plants do not struggle to reach out for more sunlight, instead, they have adapted to prosper in their low light condition. This is resourcefulness at its best. One thing is to seek out better conditions in order to function better and be more productive. But in a situation where you are totally restricted or disadvantaged from seeking better opportunities what will you do? How do you make the best use of your night?

Rejection is like a night period. A period when you can't do much. A period of limited options. A period when you must learn to be contented.

Just like that plant that has learnt to adapt, you must adapt. In your night you must find day. You must make use of the little you have to achieve more.

There are nights that you have to reach out for more, like those plants reaching out for sunlight and in the process increase their growth. That extra effort that takes you out of your comfort zone is very vital in the journey you make towards success and happiness. There are people who will always want to feel relaxed without making efforts to save their lives, except they experience rejection. Rejection is like a night period. You need that experience to be able to reconnect with your inner self and deal with your shits.

There is also the process of making do with the limited resources you have. There are those plants that would rather stay back in their night situation and absence of light and make do with what they have. They don't struggle to get sunlight. They just become contented with what available resources they have. This is also true. Some people do not understand the meaning of contentment until they face rejection. There are people who are naturally wasteful. They just sit around and enjoy being spoon-fed and as they do, they also waste it. Rejection pushes them to learn the act of preservation. They come to terms with limited resources and learn not to waste. Much progress is made in this situation.

Knowing how to survive during such times of darkness in your life is very paramount to your overall happiness. Rejection is not all negative. When the night comes, you create your light and make silent progress.

CHAPTER TEN

ISOLATION HELPS GROWTH

ISOLATION HELPS GROWTH

Ideally, you really don't require too many people around you. The larger the crowd around you the greater your commitment level. Commitment drains you. Having to satisfy too many people will not only drain you, it will also leave you frustrated and eventually, you will end up being despised. In truth you cannot make everybody happy.

You should be smart enough to know the sound of nuisance alarm. Whenever, somebody starts giving you signal that you are becoming a nuisance, pay attention and do the needful.

I will not go through the stress of listing the various ways that people show you signs that you are a nuisance.

In my personal life, one of the sounds I have become accustomed to is the sound of nuisance alarm. I can even hear the sound in my sleep state.

There is a need to understand that people always

face certain personal crises and at some point would need their "Me" time unattended by anybody.

It might not always be because of a so-called "me" time. It might also be because they don't want you occupying a major aspect of their lives. If you are not attentive you might be getting too close without seeing that they are trying to keep you off their lives.

It doesn't make them bad people. Truth is that we all do it. There have been times I have ejected some people from my life. In like manner people have also done the same to me. It is a legitimate action. The issue here is that you should know when somebody is doing that, to avoid making a mess of yourself, in your bid to remain in their life.

Watch those you call friends closely. Read the signs. Discern the sound and know when you have become a nuisance. Walk.

Your life does not depend on anybody but yourself. You won't know this until you survive a rejection and then you would come to the realization that you really didn't need that person to be happy. All you need to be happy is yourself. You need to find out how to make yourself happy without having to solicit for happiness from other people. The moment you depend on someone else to make you happy, you have already laid the foundation for emotional slavery.

Rejection breaks people down so much because they fail to see beyond the rejection. They get so fixated on the object or person of interest, that they convince themselves that they are incomplete unless the object or person of interest takes a pivotal role in their lives.

In reality, rejection opens your eyes to a life of independence. Many people who became more successful and relevant to humanity, didn't get to that point until they experienced a major rejection. After their rejection, they involuntarily went into survival mode, only to discover that there was so much power and strength within them – so much abilities to do the impossible.

Some people became founders of great companies only after their rejection experiences. There are people who found love after they were rejected by the people they were obsessed with. At the moment of rejection, you might want to believe that your life has ended, but no. It marks the beginning of a new chapter in your life.

Take the experience of Adele the musician for instance. Her musical career moved in leaps and bounds after her rejection experience. She channeled all that energy she was directing towards a man to her music. According to her, that experience became an inspiration for most of her songs. She didn't sit at a spot to whine. She rather discovered something within her – that she could actually live without him. She learnt to find happiness without depending on anybody.

Rejection saves you from the burden of multiple commitments. Nothing can be so draining as having to meet up with multiple commitments. You end up trying to please, be available, give your time, energy and resources to different people. This is actually expensive. Duplicity of efforts, can drain you more than anything. In addition to the commitment you owe others, there are also commitments you owe yourself.

Some people get to that pathetic point where they neglect themselves. All they are consumed with is how to meet up with the expectations of other people. Rejection jerks you back to reality to see that you matter more than any other person. In life, your happiness and comfort is top priority. Every other person is secondary – sadly, some people never get to know this until a traumatic incident of rejection occurs in their lives.

When you are in isolation, you start thinking about you. All that matters to you at that point is how to survive and be happy. You spend most of your time thinking of how to improve your condition. Growth happens under that atmosphere. This is because all the conditions needed for growth will be concentrated on you. Great dreams and ideas are usually birthed in moments and times of isolation. In isolation, you have no choice than to be silent and hear your own voice. This is unlike the voice of too many people that fills your ears when you have so many people around you. The voice of too many people brings comes confusion. You are bound to hear fear, discouragement, condemnation, envy, hate etc. you hardly know what to listen to. You find yourself struggling to stay focused. That is not how growth happens. All the little distractions that comes with the crowd can hinder or slow your growth.

When you are rejected and driven back to isolation, your mind starts suggesting alternatives to you. Without that rejection experience, you may never know that there are alternatives. Most people who want to harm themselves as a result of rejection, do that because they are ignorant of the fact that there are alternatives and that nobody is truly indispensable.

In your place of isolation, you are forced to put your mind to work, because self-preservation is an intrinsic nature. Humans have the ability to find means and ways of survival.

In isolation, you are not interested in pleasing

any other person but you. Everything you possess will be maximized to satisfaction.

CHAPTER ELEVEN

SELF-VALIDATION

SELF-VALIDATION

One power you should never give to anybody in life, is the power to validate you. You should be your own validation.

People who hurt more from rejection, hurt because they expected validation from other people. When you start building your self-esteem, you will understand the need to validate yourself. If you don't validate yourself, you will be giving people bullets to shoot you.

Expecting them to validate you, means they can choose to belittle you whenever they feel like. This will give them unlimited control over you. They can manipulate you for selfish reasons and sometimes talk you down, just to remind you that they still have control over you.

If you will ever be happy in life, then you must validate yourself. If you have learnt to validate yourself, people's rejection won't bother you at all. You will not be scared to hear "no". This is because you are in total control of your life. You will not find it difficult letting people off your life.

Why we maintain undue sentimentality is because we don't want to lose friends or family. Even when they are messing us up, we accommodate and sponsor our own misery.

Two months after I said goodbye to my first marriage experience, an Ex friend chatted me up on Facebook. We were colleagues. He was what I would call my best friend at that time. I know a couple of decisions I took based on his influence.

I was about a year ahead of him in Theological school and we served in the same ministerial district. In the course of our friendship, he betrayed me twice, but I let it go. Maybe I didn't actually let it go. As my friend, he was privy to my marital travails. He didn't hear, he saw with his eyes.

I will be the last person to demonize my estranged wife, because I made the choice of marrying her, myself. I have always maintained that it was an incompatibility problem - a case of forcing a square peg into a round hole. It didn't mean any of us was bad, it was just that we didn't fit into each other. The attendant pains and emotional/psychological trauma that I went through was a natural consequence of forcing a square peg into an unfitting hole it comes with bruises, which was my experience.

This my friend knew everything. In fact my marriage began to affect my productivity and he knew about it. He was older but unmarried. I was also In the know about his own relationship. I told him when I wanted to walk. He tried to dissuade me. I paid no heed, especially since he wasn't wearing my shoes. I walked.

When he chatted me up on Facebook, he was asking me why I left my marriage. I tried to be respectful in my response to him until he said: "Your wife is your demon that you should fight, you need to go back to your wife and fight your demon until you win. By walking out, you have accepted defeat."

I quickly told him that I preferred the defeat and I am happy with the defeat and I don't want to hear anything about it from him again. He should allow me to deal with my defeat, but first he should go and marry his own wife and start fighting his own demon, since a wife is now a demon. At least I have fought and failed, he should fight his own. That was the last chat I had with him and I cut him off my life totally.

You see, there are people always parading themselves as friends and family. They see you in pain, they won't do anything to help your life. The moment you decide to walk out of discomfort, they become very interested in your matter and start giving you "Ahitophelic" counsel on how to stick with pain.

Such people do not have your interest at heart. I found out that you don't need crowd in your life. You just need a few people who are sensible enough to want your happiness.

If you keep waiting for people to validate your happiness, you will die. I will not come to you for validation. I validate myself. I know what is good for me and I go for it regardless of who is not in support.

I will not empower anybody to hold me to ransom. Never.

CHAPTER TWELVE

BENEFITS OF REJECTION

BENEFITS OF REJECTION

Rejection opens your eyes to your own abilities and resources.

Most times we live lives where we depend fully on other people. When we are rejected and we survive it, we are made aware that we can actually stand on our own. It takes just time for you to look back and realize that those things you thought you couldn't do without, you could actually do without them.

Within every human are abilities and resources. Sometimes you don't know what you can do until you face rejection. When all hope is supposedly lost, then you start exploring all that is within you.

The things in your life that you neglect, rejection draws your attention to them. It is like having two phones and paying more attention to one. You will never know how important the second phone is, until something happens to the preferred phone and you have no other way of reaching out except you use the second phone.

Many people never knew they could love themselves until they were rejected by those on whose love they were dependent. It was at that point that they began to treat themselves better. They learnt to love themselves without being needy of external love. Just as I said in my book - Emotional Insurance, love is collaboration. You should love yourself first before partnering with someone else in love. People who have not mastered self-love perform badly in love relationships. They are the type who are willing to harm themselves for others. They are also the type who want to harm other people. You wouldn't need all that if you loved yourself.

Perhaps, I should add, that people struggle with rejection because they fail to realize that after rejection, they still have themselves. You should never reject yourself. After every other person has abandoned you, you still have yourself and that's all that matters.

When somebody says he/she won't be of help to you, it will force you to see that you have your own resources that are lying dormant. Without rejection, you may never come to that point where you see the resources in you. You will live all your life depending on other people or everything.

Rejection opens your eyes to the world of alternatives.

Rejection is always set to burst your bubbles by showing you that there is always an alternative. There are many routes to that destination. One of the limiting ideas that people form is that they won't find something/someone else or even better. This is a pathetic lie. You mustn't use that opportunity. There are other opportunities. That's how life works.

The person rejecting you is not the only human on earth. I know that in your moment of desperation, you will think that he/she is the only person on earth. You will be tempted to believe that he/she is custom-made for you. This is one of the beliefs that makes rejection painful. You will convince yourself that there will never be anyone like that person. It is also a lie. People abound everywhere. How many have you met? You cannot possibly sit in your obscure location and assume that you have met all there is to humans. It is sad when people say things like, "all men are evil" or "all women are evil". How many have you met in your life time?

Even family members can be replaced. Family is not usually about blood. It is about those who care and have your interest at heart. We have seen parents kill children and vice versa. We have seen siblings harm one another. Blood didn't prevent them from harming themselves. So, it is beyond blood.

The job opportunity you miss today is not the only opportunity in the world. The career support you lost is not the only one you can get. In fact when you can no longer get the support of people, then go ahead and support yourself.

When rejection occurs, it shows that a door has closed, naturally, as humans, we would seek alternatives. Yes, we seek it after the door has been closed. The wisest people prepare the alternative before the rejection.

There is nobody or nothing that you cannot live without. Life is within you. When you understand that there are alternatives, you will stop beating yourself or being scared of rejection. Get yourself prepared to use other alternatives. I always say to people that I believe so much in alternatives. When you shut a door before me, I just move on and open the next door.

Limitation mentality can keep you in captivity until you break free. The greatest people you see today have experienced the worst rejections, but they came out stronger. What that should tell you is that alternatives abound. You just have to be willing to let go. Be willing to accept the rejection and move on. Each moment you spend wallowing in self-pity is time wasted. You can channel that energy into seeking the next alternative for your happiness.

It reveals your inner strength.

Sometimes you don't know what you can handle until you are the only person you've got. That moment when everybody abandons you and you have no choice than to fight your demons all alone. It doesn't mean that anyone is an island. It just shows that you can make considerable progress on your own.

Before rejection occurs, most people will think that they can't survive on their own. Think about those people who rejected you in the past. At that time you thought you would not survive it, but you did survive it and here you are, today. The truth is that the only person you can't live without is you.

We tend to underestimate ourselves a lot. We have more power than we have been taught. When you are experiencing rejection, your life enters survival mode and the instincts of self-preservation will come to play. If you are willing to survive that rejection, you will harness the power within you and make progress.

You really can do so much on your own, without outside help. People sit down and keep hoping for a certain "destiny helper" to come their way. Most of such people will stay at that spot for a very long time. It takes rejection for some people to realize that they really can do much on their own.

When it occurs to you that you have nobody, the natural thing for you to do is to roll up your sleeves and take charge of your life. After going through rejection, it occurs to you that you didn't need that person to survive. You survived on your own.

You will never know this strength if you don't experience rejection. It is like saying, "stop being dependent". Rejection shows you that what you seek from others, you can actually find within you.

Sometimes when people are saying no to you, it is call to look inward. When the people you expect validation from disappoint you, when they talk you down, who do you run to? Of course you run to yourself and find support. You should never give up on yourself, even if everybody does. You are the best you have got.

When rejection is coming, you will feel like you will die. But, after it has happened you will see yourself breathing. You didn't die. You are still alive. Then go ahead and live. It shows you have strength. Like they say, "what doesn't kill you, makes you stronger".

Rejection sets you on the path to Self.

Rejection would most times direct your focus from people to yourself. It helps you to start seeing the abilities in yourself that you never paid attention to.

The concept of "self" is one that has not enjoyed much honest teaching and attention. We tend to see "self" as something negative. Perhaps, it is because we are taught from childhood that selfishness is bad. This makes us shudder every time "Self" is mentioned. We just imagine that there is something negative about self.

The truth that needs to be said is that self is the basis for a better relationship with others. How do you relate fine with a person who is mentally or emotionally unstable? Does that not show you that people need to pay attention to self? It is sad, but, most people pay very little attention to self. They depend on other people for almost everything. They hardly ever explore the immeasurable power of self and the benefits it brings.

When rejection comes, people are forced to fall back to self. Only then do they begin to see what they have been missing all along. You can have a very amazing relationship with yourself, to the exclusion of every other person. This involves learning to understand yourself and knowing how your mind works.

We are not all the same. We are unique in our ways. It is therefore imperative that we understand ourselves. I have found that, it often takes a very traumatic experience to set us on the path to self-awareness. This is perhaps one interesting aspect of traumatic experiences. They push you off the edge to the point where all you've got is you.

You will have no choice but to start studying and understanding yourself. It comes to you as a last resort. You are at that point where you have no one else to run to. So, you run to self and find succor. Then, you begin to learn what self-love is. Unfortunately, some people practice selfishness and call it self-love. Selfishness means finding your happiness first, at the expense of other people. Which means you can cause people pain in other to make yourself happy. Self-love means putting your happiness first, by making legitimate effort to be happy. In this case you are not causing anybody pain but you are focusing on your happiness first before others. While you are making yourself happy, you are not causing pain to others. When you succeed at self-love, you will be able to practice people-love. The love you give others is always an extension of the love you have for yourself.

With rejection, comes that push you need to focus on self and benefit from all it has to offer. So many people will never know how to rely on themselves if they never had rejection experiences.

When people reject you, they lose their power over you.

You see, we always act and behave well when we are expecting something from people. There is an unconscious effort to conform to them. Unknowingly, we empower them over us and grovel on our knees and pander to their whims and caprices. We do all these because there is something we are expecting.

Hardly, will you see someone making a request arrogantly. We are often making requests with a sense of humility so as to appeal to the sympathetic personality of our benefactor. We see them as saviors – financial, career, emotional, etc. All these changes the moment they say no to us. Something crumbles. All that throne we have built in our head and enthroned them, crashes and we dethrone them in our head. They lose that power they had over us.

Have you seen where rich people scam poor people? This is what happens. The poor expects a favour from the rich. The rich makes a promise. In the process the rich requests that the poor does something. Without making much fuss, the poor will oblige the rich. In some cases, he/she might be asked to bring money or hand over some personal possession. The poor isn't thinking, because he/she is fixated on what he would gain from the rich man. It continues until one day he finds out that the rich man is not willing to help. At that point it is already late. The rejection has occurred, but, in addition, he has also been scammed of the little he has. Expectation brings disappointment. If you don't expect you will not be disappointed. From the analogy above, you can see how the rich had power or influence over the poor. That power will not last. The moment the rejection is completed, the power becomes lost.

Romantically speaking, people also lose power over those they reject. From personal experience, I know ladies who have been interested in me at some point, but, I wasn't interested in them. Anything I desired at that time they would have given to me. If I said jump, they would jump. But, the moment I said a definitive "no" to their request for a relationship, everything changed. I lost that power over them.

They became free. I love the fact that they got back their power. Giving anybody power over you is not healthy. If you give power to the wrong people, they would use it against you.

When rejection occurs it gives you the opportunity to take back your power and become free. You no longer care about that person's feelings or satisfaction. It also takes you out of vulnerability. Some people, in their bid to get certain things in life, allow themselves to become vulnerable. This vulnerability increases their desperation. It is wise not to go after or expect things that are clearly out of your control.

When people have rejected you, there will be no need to please them any longer. All that matters to you will be your own happiness. You find freedom and power.

CONCLUSION

In reality, rejection isn't the problem. Rejection is a reality that we must all accept. The pain of rejection is made worse by a negative self-esteem and dependency mentality. How we react to rejection is what will either empower it against us or reduce its impact on us.

There is not much you can do to avoid rejection but there is so much you can do to minimize how it affects you.

One truth that you should know is that allowing people the power to reject you, helps you to know those who really want you, not those who are being with you because you are influencing them to. Allow people to take independent decisions. If somebody is with you because you are pulling manipulative stunts, it will not last for long. They will get tired and want out. It doesn't matter how long, they will leave you.

Rejection is a beautiful thing in disguise. It reveals to you how much you can do without other people. It shows you that you are the most important person in your own life. Most importantly, you will understand that brooding and depressing yourself over rejection, is double tragedy. It is like harming yourself twice. It is already enough that you have been rejected. You don't have to make it worse by being angry, sad or resentful towards yourself and those who rejected you. It is wasted emotions to do that.

When you are rejected, it calls for friendship with self. You should fall back on yourself and stand by yourself. Don't make it harder than it is by hating yourself. When you do that you will be causing more harm to yourself.

We must embrace rejection, understand it and then win the battle over it. When you are done winning this battle, it will lose its hold over you. Then you will begin to enjoy true freedom, knowing that you are not depending or hoping on anybody to validate or make you happy. When people say "no" it will no longer hurt you. You will receive it thankfully and move on.

Thank you for buying and reading this book. I hope it was helpful.

If you desire personal counseling, coaching or therapy, contact me on +2348107607613 or mail me at aletheacounsellinghouse@gmail.com

Printed in Great Britain
by Amazon